♥
_____

With Love

Also by Ruby M. Harmon

Poetic Moves While Doctoring
Being in Two Volumes

With Love

Poems by
Ruby M. Harmon

Photos by
Ruby M. Harmon
Collages by
Walter Gray Lamb

Bleeding Heart/The Paul Collection

POETIC
MOVES
PUBLISHING
New York

© Copyright 2010 by Ruby M. Harmon

Photos © Copyright 2010
by Ruby M. Harmon
Collages © Copyright 2010
by Walter Gray Lamb, used by permission

All rights reserved. Printed in the United States of America. No part of this book may be transmitted or reproduced by any means, electronic or mechanical, without written permission of the author or publisher, except for quotations included in reviews.

ISBN 10: 0-9824277-1-9
ISBN 13: 978-0-9824277-1-2

Published by Poetic Moves Publishing
P.O. Box 630106
Bronx, NY 10463

Book and cover design by Walter Gray Lamb

Table of Contents

9. Petit Bateau
10. Like Love
11. Sometimes, Just Sometimes
12. Honey to Me
13. Student Teacher
14. Healing #3
15. Yearning
16. Wishing You Here #2
17. Long
18. *And with my Heart*
19. Love #2
20. Ma Coccinelle
21. Body
22. Even
23. For Lovers
24. You
25. Mused
26. To Mom
27. *Rose #7*
28. Mementos
29. L'Écrivain
30. Irresistible
31. Love
32. Bliss
33. Heart to Heart
34. Love Healing
35. Late Night Driving
36. *Those Lips... Hers*
37. Knowing II
38. He Said, She Said
39. He and She III
40. Reminders II
41. Healing
42. Cold
43. Wishing You Here
44. Sans Souci
45. *Heartfelt Rose*
46. For Eign

♥

48. Love-Joy
49. Ode to Moses and Edna
50. To Read the Words
52. Labor of Love
53. Simply You
54. *Everyman, I will go with Thee*
55. He and She II
56. Surprisingly You
57. Daffodil
58. Ours to Keep
59. Engaged
60. He and She I
61. Teenage Rant and Praise
62. Connected
63. *Mother and Child, sand painting, Nigeria*
64. Letters to My Mother
65. If, But for One Breath
66. Comfort Two
67. Mother and Son
68. Refuge
69. After the Party
70. Knowing
71. In Awe of Greatness
72. *Classic No. 5*
73. Knowing You
74. Questioning You, Questioning Me
75. 27 Years
76. Plain
77. First Kiss
78. Spotted Beauty
79. He and She IV
80. Bleeding Heart
81. *Hearts on a String/ The Paul Collection*
82. Wishing Well
83. The Miracle of You

84. Comfort
85. Hope
86. Connected Two
87. Life 2
88. Thoughts
89. He and She V
90. *The Learning Tree*
91. Reminders
92. Love 3
93. Retreat
94. Taste
95. He and She I
96. Encounters
97. Caressed by You
98. Untitled II
99. The Difference
100. Living You
101. *Six Roses*
102. Keepsake
104. Acknowledgements

♥
―――

Dedication As always, to Queen Mary, my mother, who first loved me…

To love and positivity

PETIT BATEAU

I dreamt of you last night
I dreamt of us last night
I dreamt of me last night

Caress my troubles in your embrace
Undo each insurmountable height
Believe me capable in spirit

Your arms are my petit bateau
Rocking away anguish
Floating placidly on clear waters
Comforting without even knowing
We, two, voyaging to foreign places

Place your anchor
Near to my heart
For there protected
Our like stays firm

So vivid in my dreams
When morning awakens
My ship has sailed
Untouchable but seen

LIKE LOVE

From like
True love
Turns
Unfolds
Evolves
Learns
Vibrates
To like

SOMETIMES, JUST SOMETIMES

Sometimes, you know
I sense
My heart stretched
Thin, like muslin—
Minute squares of fine woven thread

And
Sometimes, you see
Tiny drops of eye water
Trickle down
From canthus to lips

The taste salty
On my tongue
As I open my mouth
To scream
Out the hurt

And
Sometimes, just sometimes
I feel your sweet breath
Blowing the hurt far, far away

HONEY TO ME

Your love
To me
Is like honey
Straight from the comb—
Golden
Rich
Sticky
Pure
Unadulterated sweetness

STUDENT TEACHER

What if someone spoke of you
Disparagingly;
Discouraged your innate desire
To excel;
Concocted ploys to keep you down
Contorted words that oppressed
Pointed a finger and dared you to rebel
Even belittled the few choices you made?
Yet you still loved and cared and gave
Refusing to reciprocate the negativity,
Refusing to abide by their destructive laws

What if you were only ten years old?

Who would be the teacher?

Who would be the pupil?

HEALING #3

Something tells me our meeting was meant to be
More than simply
Two sharing words
Sharing
Something tells me our words
Will construct
Bridges
To unite man
Kind, woman
Kind words
To heal
One
People
Something tells me
As one we
Will someday
Speak
Nonverbally
Share openly
Casting "-isms" aside

Won't that be something?

YEARNING

My arms yearn for your embrace
Singularly warm
Unique
Full
Comforting
Loving

My memory converts it
To
Plural
Encompassing
Whole
Oneness.

WISHING YOU HERE #2

This day	each part of me wants you
Here	in words
Minimizing	
The distance	of oceans, lands, and sky
As if	my hands could hold
What separates us	deep in its palm
	And touch the realness
	of you,
	If only the mind
Would acquiesce	would paint you
Simply	in memories
Willingly	drawing the contours
	of the you
	I once embraced
Each part of me	
Could feel	each part of me could speak
You, here	gratefully in words

LONG

Ago   we
spoke of love hidden
in notes orchestrated on paper
and now, we play long solos and
sonatas with brass, timbales, harps
oboes, cellos, violas, and voices
myriad voices proclaiming and
harmonizing our refreshing
melodies—mere reflect-
ions of love played
out in song

LOVE #2

shields
words.
fingers caress
compassionately

look

how unconditional hate
isn't.

MA COCCINELLE

You're like a ladybug, he'd say
Leaving me blushing
Yet now knowing why

Perhaps in thinking
I may have saved his soft-petaled roses
Their downfall
Or even intrigued him
In some unspoken way

And after all these years
Of our union
Only now, do I ponder the comparison
For, my love, an entomologist
Adores the tiny creatures
                    That many deem nuisances

So, I guess, I'm delighted
That my comparison is not to a flea

BODY

B– BATHE YOURSELF IN LOVE AND POSITIVITY.
O– OH! AWAKEN TO YOUR POTENTIAL!
D– DEMAND ONLY THE BEST. YOU DESERVE IT!
Y– YOU ARE UNIQUE. AN AMAZING CREATION. LET YOUR BODY RELISH IN THIS REALITY.

EVEN

Even if love lay prostrate before you,
Would you see it?
Or trip over its improvised form?
Would its melody convince
Finding its niche deep inside?
Would the lyrics waltz or salsa
Partnered with your essence?

The language of love knows its place
Within you.
So germane to your spirit
And yet you refuse its embrace.
Open your arms
And accept its warmth
Open your eyes
And savor its brilliance.

FOR LOVERS

they wondered why we stood
so close apart
our spaces intersecting

your arc, a blue-green opal
mine, a brilliant topaz
ours together, rich and vibrant

iridescent
words incubating between our lips
pressed close together

we tasted syllables
sweet and bitter

nothing seemed
to break the spell cast
between us

complex, this close

distance

we kept our moments
telling everyone who dared
listen to our contradictions

love was defining
our actions

YOU

There's more to you than just tattoos:
  there's depth and humor
  wit and intelligence
    the way your hand comforts
    that stance, holding your body
    just so
  the ease with which you embrace challenges
  that gentle spirit you so firmly assert
    quiet confidence that need not threaten others
  your acceptance of mistakes
  yours and mine.

I am so proud to know you;
to be
a part of your evolving world.
I accept my place with you,
never knowing what life has in store for us.
I enjoy our partnering
with its ups, downs, and middle ground.

MUSED

Seemingly, quiet, he stared
His yet unknown secret
Tucked away in her heart

Together, they dove deeper and deeper
The ocean washing their misaligned bodies
The waves cascading, cleansing, renewing

Her smile was the balm to his soul
Her hand undoing portals long forgotten
His muse, he pondered…
Yet, her magical stillness and mystique
Questioned his very being

Their bodies flamboyantly dividing water
Dancing elementally, accenting nature

He had dreamt of moments like these
The paradox of stillness in motion

He enjoyed their asymmetry and
She…the same

TO MOM

My admiration for you is but a mere token of gratitude
For having birthed me
Against stacking odds

Believing my life too precious
And had to be lived
Guiding and directing
Even in times of uncertainty

My love for you is gentle and petaled
As beautiful as a summer's rose
You, who understood me
Loved me, clothed me, taught me

Yes, I chose you
And rightfully so
And now I thank you

For being you—the rock
The strength, the glue
The comfort, the one that I adore

The lady with the might.

MEMENTOS

"You know," she whispered
"What love is?"

It's throwing me a chocolate kiss with ribbons attached
It's massaging that one spot that envelopes my troubles
It's fully and intentionally hugging
Watching the sun slip under a pink iridescent sky

It's knowing my faults and loving me nonetheless
It's hot tea with the honey just right
It's embracing life, holding on
Then letting go at the right moment

It's those silly jokes that force a laugh

It's hate turned on its head and rearranged
It's impatience dispelled, anger dissipated
Violence silence, jealously crushed, and
Rage controlled

It's bare-boned, unadulterated, unsugarcoated
Living-life-to-the-fullest
Caring not to hurt yourself or others

It's thanking you for walking alongside me
…even when my strength faltered.

L'ECRIVAIN

I miss you!
Your surprising nightly calls at three,
holding my head gently between
two palms.
We laying as one,
writing together on paper.
You, knower of my deepest core.
Words flowed rivers
endlessly inked.
Waves caressed shores.
We walked arms linked
through rainy nights on Crownhill,
relishing the rain, fresh on our cheeks.
Even laughed after the first kiss
behind the bleachers,
knees wobbling. The first touch.
How we traveled through time.

Even now, you echo my private thoughts.
My eyes devour
our meetings, etched on paper.

Where are you, my love?
My nib awaits your gentle
often-persistent nudge.

IRRESISTIBLE

What's in those eyes
that pierce as deeply
as the sun's glare?

Skin that welcomes
fingers in long strides
hands cupping a shoulder.
Tenderly, lips brush cheeks

A whisper

within ear's reach.
The words lovingly allow
mouths to meet
a deep dimpled you.

What's in those eyes
that makes loving
you so irresistible?

LOVE

"I love you," she said
all of three years old.
Reaching for my walker
She climbed under the bars,
grabbed my legs, hugging tightly.
"I love you too, baby."
This was our routine
every night
just before bedtime.
Little did she know,
those words kept me
going.

BLISS

something inside whispers sweet
like cotton candy to kids
riding the merry-go-round
glistening smiles
laughing uncontrollably

        something inside sings
        lyrics woven magically
        nurturing
        caressing
        crevices left untended

something inside leaves
            the recipient
            ecstatically
            pleased!

HEART TO HEART

What inspires me to write
Of you
Stronger
Beautiful
Healing

Our hearts speak
To your heart
Connected in prayer
Soothing your hurt
As a salve would a wound

We sing
In thanksgiving
Of you
Healing beautifully
Blessed from above

LOVE HEALING

Joy in my heart
Resounding, rejoicing
Beating jubilantly
Undeterred by grief

Let me share
This peace uplifting
Joy in my soul
Unraveling the cornered sorrow
Burrowed shallow

Sing praises
Live life fully
Arms raised high, embracing the world

Spread love in childlike measure
Bursting forth in healing flames
Celebrating the joy within
Inadvertently,
       Healing the world, though one.

LATE-NIGHT DRIVING

Seated inside you
Our movements become one
Rolling
Down dark winding roads

You know,
These late-night drives deliciously leave me
Wanting more

Exhilarating enough

To make our hairs stand on end
As we meander
Through highs and lows
Basking in the cool night air's refreshing touch

The moon peeks its head forward
Nodding at our playful romp

Seated in you
Driving even thirty miles per hour
My heart laughs
Loudly
One beat at a time

KNOWING II

We knew
from the first meeting:
Our eyes met
danced about each other
lips bantered with others

Formalities.

We knew then,
that the second
meeting would be
more telling.
We felt
the moment our eyes
locked in a glance.

HE SAID, SHE SAID

"…Love the way your fingers caress
the indent of my neck.
Love the way your words
wrap ever so gently.
The way the silence lingers,
welcomed between us,"
He said

"I love way we become
lost and serene;
simple pleasures of our love.
I love the way…" she said
He said "…love lingers comfortably
In our midst."

HE AND SHE III

"You've never understood me," she muttered
Words emoting from within her burka
Hennaed hands reaching toward his shoulder

A step away from cultural mores,
How dare she?

Not frightened by his look of stupefaction and horror
The burka removed
Tears revealed,
      A look of pain on her face

He now speechless
Hands placed over his ears
As tears softened his face
Filling prideful lines so strategically engraved

In disbelief, he stared
Then screamed, " Woman, how dare you?'

But she knew
In truth
The tears had softened his heart.

REMINDERS II

On some cold mornings
I've missed the touch
Of one
Lightly against my back
Whispering against my cheek

Frosty-lipped

The chill tiptoes
Lightly against my back

On some cold mornings

Whistling against the window pane
Inviting a shiver

Reminders
That indeed, I'm alive

HEALING

You entered
Welcomed into my belly
Bedrocked,
emotionally cuddled.
See,
how
calmly you lay prostrate,
how compliant the gusts of wind.
Hush, be still.
Let time mend
your ache.

COLD

I feel so cold
without you
here.
Is it that
I have become so attached
to your warmth?

WISHING YOU HERE

This day   each part of me wants you
Here   in words
Minimizing
The distance   of oceans, lands, and sky

Wishing   my hand could hold
What separates us   deep in its palm
                    And touch the realness
                    Of you,
This day   as if the mind
Would acquiesce   would paint you
Simply   in memories
Willingly
                    Drawing the contours of the you
                    I once embraced

This day   each part of me feels you
Here   in words

SANS SOUCI

So tenderly,
You cup my face
Robust lips skim my cheeks
Your eyes drink up
All of me
Aphrodisiac
Hear me calling you
Feel my words tugging
Rapping ever so faintly
Let your arms enclose me
In your warm embrace
Completely
Let's indulge our passion…
Sans souci

FOR EIGN

I shall tell them:

I have met my love
True, loyal, foreign
To them
She: graceful, understanding, adventurous.

I remember, as a child,
The only son
Favored and nurtured.
The customs inculcated.
Our women shrouded, their beauty
Wanting behind heavy, dark respect;
Their faint laughter when seated
Together.
And we men, dared not stare
Openly.
Imagination never shared
Knowing the risk of unwed touch.

♥

I shall tell them:

I have found her, habibi.
Favoring, nurturing me.
Our words weave tapestries, rich
Our sounds strum harmonies.
If only you could hear…

I do not question her desire
Not to don the hijab;
Her beauty proudly displayed
Foreign to them, who judge character not
from within,
Who see a woman's worth with eyes steeped in
traditional mores.

She has been my partner
Arab–non-Arab.
She has been my pillar, my reason

And I am still your son
Being nurtured by another
Whose ways must seem so foreign
To you

LOVE-JOY

And what of this love
That you have welcomed so graciously
That leaves your mind topsy-turvy
Weaving boldly
Displayed as that twinkle in your eyes
And enlightened glow on your cheeks?

What of the joy
That radiates in your eyes
And emanates from your pores
There for all to see?

Your blissful smile tells all

This love speaks in syllables
Infectious
Poetically knitted with receptive lips
Recited openly

How exciting that this love can be
More than just romance alone

ODE TO MOSES AND EDNA

"Sit, Edna," he said wearily
Leaving a space carved out
In his homemade rattan rocker
Sit.
And in that moment
Years of toting
Firewood and water vanished
Labor seemed lighter
In one simple utterance

We'd both courted time
Engraved lines well sewn
In the melanin
But he knew just how
To circle his palm
Embracing the roundness
Defining my shoulder
Massaging ever so slowly my back
Slowly, not because of age
But because of skill: he just knew
These moments of tenderness
Was why
I loved him so

Sit, he'd say
And I knew
That our special moments
Would unfold naturally.

TO READ THE WORDS

Dear Margaret,
It's been years since we spoke
You never write and since I don't have a phone
    I never call.
This may be my last letter to you
    But I trust that you are well.
Love,
Mitchell

She has pretended this long
To read the words and know the letters
And though she speaks well
Enough
To read
The words have never stuck
In the recesses of her mind

In times past, leaving elementary school to
work
To feed the hungry lips
That later thanked her endlessly was common-
place
Even expected
And Mitchell would tease her because he liked
her
Even at such a young age
For that is what young boys do

♥
───────

Oh Mitchell,
If only you knew that I don't know to put pen
      To paper or recite the words written there
Your letters are all stacked neatly in my
      Favorite shoebox with ribbon trimmings
      For I treasure them all…

Back then, school was to pass the time
While we waited to work

My good friend Mildred insists it's never too late
So I've learned twenty letters and ninety words
      Including *dyslexia*
And today on my birthday
I can proudly write
My name

LABOR OF LOVE

The roundness that is her
Pushes out
With little feet kicking
Curled inside, against the liquid warmth.

And each beat,
Beats in time
Soon to face the earth
In days

This living she feels
Against her hand
Moves restless with each breath
Awaiting the inevitable
Push
With every ounce of strength
Crowning two the new joys
That came through labor

Breathing outside her womb
Against her face
Their vernix shows
That beauty comes from within
Their cries proclaim
This a labor of love.

SIMPLY YOU

Simple words I will write
To show my love
Blooming
Fuchsia petals
Plentiful thoughts I have of you
Nurturing, sacrificing, guiding
Demonstrating love in all that you do
A multitude of kisses
I bestow upon you, dearest Mother
You who encouraged me
Protected me
You who wrapped me snugly
In your warm embrace
You who bring laughter
And joy into our midst
Wonderful Mother that you are
I cherish you always

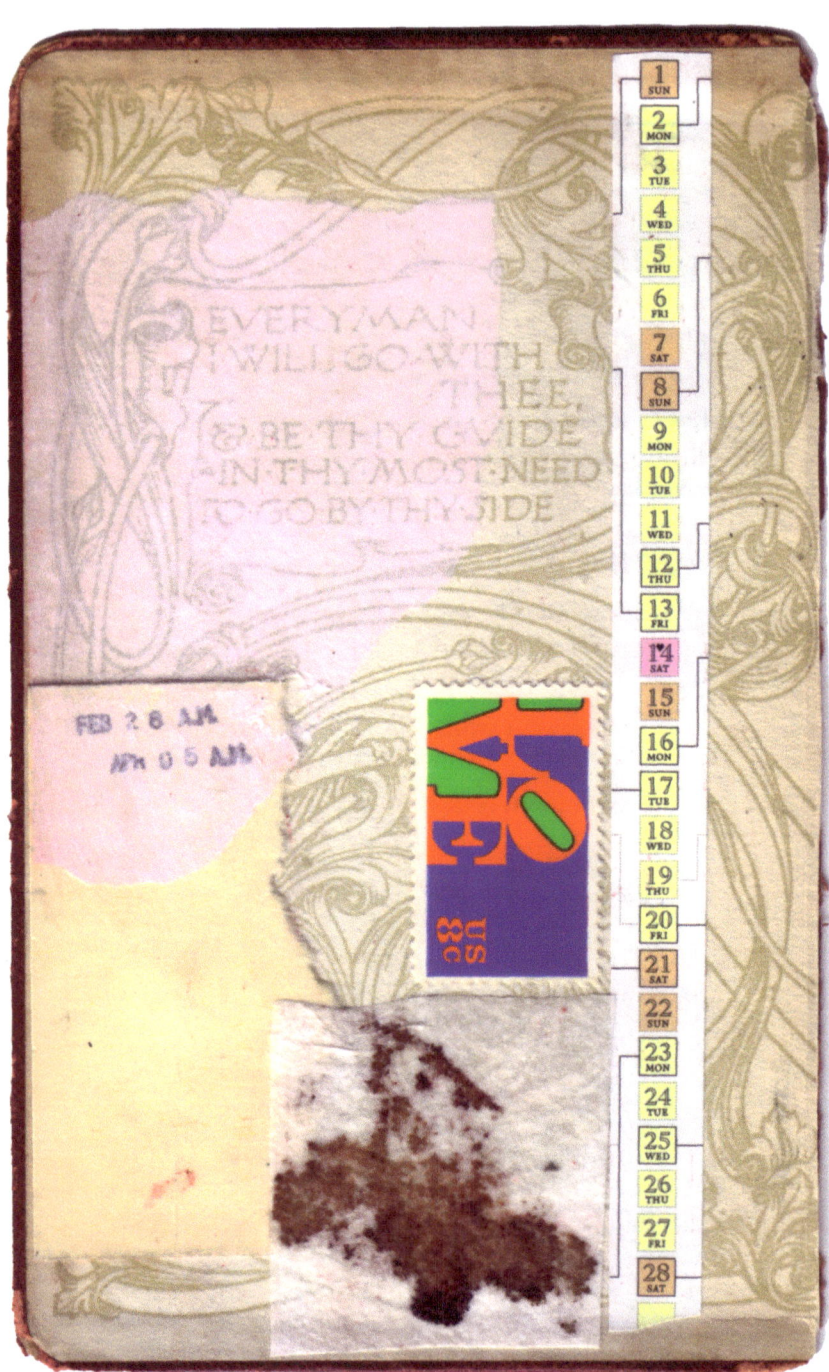

HE AND SHE II

I watched as they walked hand in hand
Almost two centuries between them

Her hat, shielding her from the truth of age
His cane, speaking volumes

They laughed,
Only they knowing the private joke laid between them

Taking slow deliberate steps
Chancing a fall

But, oh, what the hell
Life had to be lived

Proudly, as others watched
They continued their strides

Having made a date
…for pizza.

SURPRISINGLY YOU

You make my mind and body
sing
simply
just
by
being
you.

DAFFODIL

Even if I tried
to ignore you
I couldn't.
Like sunshine, brilliantly
you court my eyes
hypnotizing simply by being.

We stare
my face facing your petaled flower.

Heeding your call…
lost I am delighted
seeing in you the beauty of life.
Your melody echoes
softly
tickling my core.

OURS TO KEEP

Speak sweetly in my ear
Sonnets tenderly recited
Verses, each one calming
Fears of love unspoken
Still fiery, uncontained

Open up your heart
Keyed into mine
Forgoing inhibition
As oceans wash onto shore
Pleasurable to the eyes that behold
Under pumpkin sunsets

Hold me gingerly
Two embraced
Until silence screams loudly
Releasing pain

Our moment of freedom
Climaxed gently
Keyed in your heart and mine

ENGAGED

Engaged
She is
With ring to left fourth
Finger
Refusing party affiliation
Engrossed in stimulating discussion
With her partner, who also
Announces their intention with
Words concealed in metal around
The left fourth finger

Both engaged mutually
In words and symbol
Politically charged
Without apprehension or concern
For those preaching against
Who deserves whom

Engaged
She is
With feelings entrenched
Deep and personal
Refusing party announcements
With metal and words
Woven
And ample

HE AND SHE VI

He whispered
The words floated lightly
Evaporating the worry
Blanketing the sorrow

But the words would only stay

Temporarily

For it was she who usually knew the right words
And spoke them so easily
Embracing those in need

And now as recipient
Words alone proved inadequate
Lost in the vast void that remained

In this silent space, she knew that only
Time could diminish
The uneasiness that lingered in her consciousness

TEENAGE RANT AND PRAISE

Hey Ma,
      I am from you.
Look at me
with an attitude fiery, reminiscent of your teenage years,
so Grandma says;
With lips unrestricted
spewing out words
without a second thought
with arms in your face
gesticulating
standing shoulder to shoulder.

      Yes, I know that I'm under
      your roof. You pay the bills
      You buy my clothes, the food.
      You give me allowance
      to be feisty,
      so Grandma says.
But, Ma, I do love you
though I don't admit it.
My world would crumble
if you weren't in it.
You should see the letters

I've written over the years:
All very appreciative of you, Ma.
Honest…

CONNECTED

Imagine
Me and you
At a point
Lying connected
Life flowing from big to small
Miraculously

A hand places the clamp to cord
Forcing independence
And with ease I breathe
Thanking you

The remnant of this remains visible
On my body, the indentation about the pubis
Now a repository for lint
Or a finger placed
Jokingly

Exposed purposefully
Pierced

This tuft of tissue reminds me
How connected we were then
And how connected we still remain
Without the cord
Between us

LETTERS TO MY MOTHER

      TYSDMUREODELN   VILOYEUO

  EAJMTIE

            ÉMORNETNÉM

AGDHETUR TMROTHEO

              LEFLI À EMRÈ

I love you tremendously
Je t'aime énormément
Daughter to mother
Fille á mère

♥

IF, BUT FOR ONE BREATH—*A tribute to Daddy*

If…but for one breath,

He took his first breath
—in breathed life
A life well-lived, to the fullest measure

A man dearly loved
A man of great stature, style, and accomplishments
A statesman, the patriarch, ambassador-at-large
Indeed at-large, for he touched the lives of many
He shared a part of his life
       leaving indelible memories—
       by which we celebrate his life

We can recount the stories of his empathy undoing the pain of others
We know of periods where his empathy was misdirected…
his heart and soul being so entwined in the Liberian fabric

If, but for one breath
He were here today:
What would he say?
I love you; I miss you, let bygones be bygones

If, but for one breath,
He were here today:
What would you say?

…what would I say?
Daddy, we love you and we know that you have gone
       to a glorious utopia
          of which we can only dream…

Family tribute read at Daddy's funeral July 5, 1997, *Celebrating Daddy's Life, 1911–1997, Washington Cathedral, Washington, DC*

COMFORT TWO

Amidst the carols
She twirls the thin curls
That frame the baldness
Of her father's head

The whimper starts softly
Eased as her mouth accepts the bottles
Willingly
He, maternally, cuddles her
In the seat of his arms
Rocking and humming
Naturally
And the comfort she feels
Is what he preaches about

Innocence is sometimes a blessing…

MOTHER AND SON

The words, inaudible, cartwheel
chaotically from her mind;
her lips occasionally smiling
rebuffing my questions
unintentionally, conversing with the air.

Our last encounter was
less disturbing and so I ask her
about the incessant talking.
Raising the volume, she barks,
"I have to. I can't help it." and proceeds
with her discourse.

And he, four years old, autistic
clings to her
chest to chest
as if he can hear her chatter.

Attached,
he seeks solace with her.

Again, I call her
and she enters my world with appropriate responses
briefly. I am faced with
protecting him from her,
for his sake and hers.
I wonder how she's cared for him
all this time. I ponder
the effect of separating the two.

"It's ridiculous," she blurts.
"I don't trust them";
Smiling and conversing with no one in particular,
all the while holding her son
close to her bosom.

REFUGE

Should I stay and place
my wants among your
desires?
Seek comfort
in your eyes?
Hold time still
as we converse
telling our secrets, aches, joys,
and pains?
Should I stay and hold
your hand
feeling it completely
enclose my hand?
Should I stay and let my thoughts
romp carefree among your thoughts?
Should I trust
that
I can seek refuge here
without being
judged?

AFTER THE PARTY

Filled, I felt
    the joy overwhelmingly
        welling up, ballooning inside me
            overpowering
                and soon, my mouth would tremble
                    uncontrollably
                        with sounds bursting forth
                            loudly
                            water trickling down my cheek
                            joy and gratitude
                            too sweet to be held back

How could I not accept
    the love?
        Exuberant, energetic
            it flowed, danced, sang, whispered
                it screamed
                    radiating light from every part of me.
                        What joy!
                            Even now,
                            I savor its uniqueness.
                            I desire its permanence…

KNOWING

Reach deep inside
and know that I am
here in your speak
in your stance
in your steps
through the pains and joys
even in those trying moments
when you doubt my promise
even when you question my presence
I am always, always here
within you.

IN AWE OF GREATNESS

I smell the aroma, subtle, light, and refreshing of your presence
    see the wondrous marvels of your hands
    feel the omnipotent power of your touch
    hear the magnificent inspiration in your voice
    taste the remarkable joy so willingly spread

Intuitively, living, I know that
in my deepest, saddest,
most joyful, and happiest moments
You are there
being my strength.

KNOWING YOU

…It was as if
we had known each other
maybe twenty years or more;
the way you spoke
and the ease with which
I let your words frolic
deep in my ears
striking familiar chords.
Words that assuaged,
Tickled;
words that allowed a joy
ful tear
egress down my cheek.

I gathered the melody
note by note
and played it
privately
for days…

QUESTIONING YOU, QUESTIONING ME?

Silence isn't golden here
In this space
Of doubt and blame

Eyes locked in do-si-do
The quiet preempting the strike
Like some hyena stalking his prey

The anticipation of both
Is that of conflict
Unveiled in questions posed
And questions forged
With neither answering the claims

The moment stands still
The hyena leaps assuredly
In midair
The prey narrowly escaped

The moment thickly lingers
Checkmate.

27 YEARS

Look at me
And see twenty-seven years of our life
Shared
Equally and unequally
Lived
Blissfully and selfishly
The commitment sometimes difficult to keep

The beauty of our love
So powerful
The occasional hurt so flabbergasting
The joys so exhilarating

Wisdom has taught us
To love for the moment
To appreciate each other
Pain has taught us
To embrace change

Cognizant of life's cyclical nature
And the challenges that togetherness brings
Today we stand
Unwavering
As one

PLAIN

Facing him,   Facing her,
her lips plainly dressed,   he was flying

who would have thought
they'd kiss
so intensely.
                                          high.

FIRST KISS

His lips felt
Robust, moist
Dark purple, enclosing hers
Painted thin whispers

His cheek smooth, defined
Caressed hers.
And at that moment, it seemed her heart
Would take flight,

He sensed her apprehension
Whispering softly, the words
"Relax, my dear, relax":
It was then that her rivers overflowed
And welcomed him.

SPOTTED BEAUTY

He loved her
Skin two
Toned
Covering an essence deep in thought
And purpose
Seeing the beauty of diversity
He would embrace all that she offered
And moments would pass
The two sharing for hours…

Not once did he think her less
Than perfect
The skin to him
Merely
A thin veneer of what lay
Hidden beneath.

HE AND SHE IV

He says
His joints are as worn
As the rusty hinges of that ninety-year-old
barn.
She says
His aches speak of generations
Of lifting, picking, hauling, shucking
Carrying weight
His palms callused
His fingers curved
The right fifth severed since childhood.

He tells of working the railroads
She hums spirituals
That carried them through.
Hardships seemed a dime a dozen then
But faith fought their battles.

She quilts still at 84.
Flying geese meant more back then
Secrets locked in fabric and thread
Elusive to those who thought
Them simple.

His wrinkles are as hers:
Carved deeply
In rich mahogany skin.
He still works at 90
Picking and hauling
174 years of humbled history.

He and she
Still legends in the making.

BLEEDING HEART

Arms wide-spread
Flowered, you wear your hearts on your sleeves
Green stemmed, your fuchsia fullness causes stares
Perhaps I could watch you for hours
How your petals must make Cupid
Sing
Hearts strung
White dainty slippers balanced gracefully
Two turned upwards

The dew lingers there willingly
Your beauty indescribable
My first glance lingered, too
Mesmerized at the love you exude

What should we call you?
Your heart felt beauty entrances
My fingers gently embrace you

Too soon, you will bid us adieu:
Your hearts relinquishing
One by one

WISHING WELL

I wish to
Restore you to the vibrant you
Put the sparkle back in your eyes
Place a smile on your dispirited face
Embrace you with hope and faith
Cherish the celebrated moments

Respect your need for calm and quiet
Listen to your myriad expressions
Understand your daily struggle
Light a candle to illuminate
      Your path to wellness
Share your desire for healing
All the while
Seeking direction from the God who understands
Everything

THE MIRACLE OF YOU

Have we shown our delight
At having you back?
It seemed for a moment
That you had left us
Even you said so yourself

Oh, how we missed
Hearing your voice
Wise and learned
Sharing your life
Seeing your smile
Enjoying your laugh
Your humor so contagious

The miracle of you
Still leaves us astonished

Every day,
We sing,
"welcome back home to wide-opened arms
welcome back home to wide-opened arms"

COMFORT

And some wonder why
I chose this—
His smile
Dimpled
Despite the white coat that announced
My presence
To listen to his heart beat

The red rubber and metal
Holding his attention
Only momentarily
When out reached his hands
Tiny
Welcoming
His mother standing there
Shocked

I reached, lifting him
As would his mother

He places his head
On my shoulder

Oblivious of the whiteness
That always frightens him

His mother smiles
Noting that he is smiling
Comfort—
Ably, still

HOPE—*for Lukas*

Who are you to speak
about hope
in forgotten crevices
disguised in moments trying
to persuade
behind bolted doors
beautifully carved maple with iron handles
encouraging its opening?

Who are you to write
so beautifully
insisting hope lies in each raindrop
watering stunted growth
coaxing beautiful buds
to unfold?

Who are you to see
hope
in the eyes of an infant
wanting to live
in the words of a centenarian
in the smile of a toddler
running uninhibited?

Hope is there
in its many forms.
Reach forward and embrace it.
Feel its power surround you.
Know that its love surrounds you.

CONNECTED TWO

I am connected to God
Who is All
That is omniscient
Fearful, I need not be
Walking in the strength this allows
Gracefully
The reality of this is, oh, so magnificent!

LIFE 2

What makes life sparkle?

> A simple smile
> A heart full of laughter
> Feeling healthy in mind, body, spirit
> Uttering thanks for being
> Reaching out to someone
> The healing power of touch
> What sounds like music to your ear
> Healthy thoughts and vibrations
> Knowing you
> Being embraced by Infinite Love
> Knowing that tomorrow is a new day
> Embracing the "inner child"
> Remembering that we are truly one—
>   All connected in this amazing universe
> One people!

THOUGHTS

I thought of embracing
You
    Life is beautiful, you said
    As the words pranced
    Out of your lips
The *eff* forever engraved in this moment
Es curled resting comfortably
Beautifully ensconced
In my mind

I thought of that moment
    When we marveled at
    The fullness at the end
    Of beauty
How life framed it so

I thought of embracing you
    All the while seeing life
    In you
I thought of life
      And you
      And words
      Three words

Life is beautiful, you said…

HE AND SHE V

It felt like cotton
On his nape
Each strand bolted upright
A whispered chill lingered
Under the warmth of her palm

The soft, gentle perfumed
Hand laid there
Its tapered elegance placed
Gracefully over the bony prominence
That begged for warmth

His hand explored hers gently
Bringing it to receive words
Against his lips
And she enclosed each word
Purposefully
Carrying it within

And soon each other their hands would find
Drawn together
Held tapered and callused
Palm to palm
He and she
Letting the moments endure
Seconds, minutes, hours…

REMINDERS

On some cold mornings
I've missed the touch
Of one
Lightly against my back
Whispering against my cheeks

Frosty-lipped
The chill tiptoes
Lightly against my back

On some cold mornings
I've missed the touch
Of one
Whistling against the window pane
Inviting a shiver

Reminders
That indeed, I'm alive

LOVE 3

I relish the comfort
your love brings.
I dread the moment
when it shall fade
leaving my heart to swim
all alone…

RETREAT

The gentle touch of your fingertips
To my skin
In moments wanting
Of your caress
With lips lightly brushing
My nape
Enrapts me in this warm comfortable love

For hours, we rest just so
With no words uttered
Yet ridding our minds
Of entangled stress

In this place
This retreat
Of surrender

That omits worry and pain
I hear my name echoed tenderly
In harmony with
Yours

taste

my lips gathered words
held in a kiss
and waited
patiently for your embrace.

my hands anticipated
your subtle touch
my ears, your smell.

my eyes could taste
the moment
soon come.

HE AND SHE (I)

He sits and questions whether she'll return
Her promise etched in his memories
Remembering the times when they were one

For far away, she has gone
Without a trace, without a line

He dreams awake—
what some would call a fantasy—
of her return
but two years gone,
he must move on

She lays awake at night
If only he knew
How sleep-deprived she has become
His tender kisses had once eased the day's pain

Both he and she refusing to drop a line
To ease the hurt that left a stain

If only their pride, they would forego…
What possibilities would be revealed

ENCOUNTERS

Riding the elevator
His fingers leaped at the chance
Pushing the buttons
Watching them light up
"Hi," he said, "hi".

        Lost in another
        World, my thoughts tangled
        His eagerness distracting
        Attracting my glance
        A minute or three

We exited together
"B— basement," he said
Running, skipping.
He turned, smiling
Threw me
A kiss
Brightening my day.
How contagious his joy!
Simply reminding me to laugh, even love
Unconditionally.

CARRESSED BY YOU—*for Kalia*

Ten tiny fingers
Ten tiny toes
Delicate miracle
Of you
Mother, father

Nurtured in birth water, essentially
Caressed gently by two
Lullabies sung, serenading you
Precious one, you are beauty defined

Candles lit the day you were born
Pronouncements sent forth
Heralding your arrival, now come
Your hand reaches out
Security ensured
As three are bonded soul to soul

Your birth, a gentle miracle wrought
The embodiment of love share tenderly by two
O shine, shine bright star!
You, joy manifest beyond mere words
Your new life lies invitingly before you,

Shouting, "Welcome beloved," the world calls…

UNTITLED II

This love has just rocked my body
Leaving me unsettled
Torrential feelings
Creeping in—wanted and unwanted

Uneasiness, unfamiliar
Control banished
All too sudden
Like children playing
Unsuspectingly bending your knees
From behind with theirs

A roller coaster ride
Yet to be replicated by theme parks
Wild, unpredictable voyage

Enticing briefly
Yet each time we meet
Butterflies arrive unannounced
Preventing words from flowing freely

One image recurs
These new feelings unsettling
Dust long collected
Stirring up and wiping clean

Baring a heart
Open to being caressed
Lovingly
And passionately

THE DIFFERENCE

The difference between
Those who care and those
Who don't
Can be as simple
As wiping a brow
Or being silent
When your mouth
Wishes to speak
Loudly

LIVING YOU

Get lost in the moment
If harmless and satisfying
Wrap yourself in great feelings
Tickling all of the senses

Feel the nearness of you
See the being that is you
Taste the joy that is you
Hear the melody within you
Touch the core that lies within you
Smell the fragrance of you

Praise the Creator
Spirit uninhibited
Share your uniqueness daily
Believing yourself a gift to the world

Wrap yourself in great feelings
Celebrate and appreciate all that is you.

KEEPSAKE

keep our love
      like a
                      gentle
breeze...

Acknowledgements

Thank you to my loving family for always standing by my side and believing in me.

Thanks to my dear friends, including Vania who predicted the cover even before its inception, for being there and supporting my work.

To Walter Lamb, a gifted artist indeed! Your talents amaze me!

To Karen Tongish, for skillfully and truthfully editing the book.

Simply put, "With Love" wishes to demonstrate love in all its colors, forms, flavors and variations.

LOVE, LOVE, LOVE FULLY!

SEE IT!

FEEL IT!

BE IT!

www.ingramcontent.com/pod-product-compliance
Lightning Source LLC
Chambersburg PA
CBHW042023150426
43198CB00002B/48